That's What I Like About Me! Booklet Two: Self-Awareness to Self-Esteem

Tasha Crews

Copyright © 2023

All Rights Reserved

Dedication

To all humans who may have lost their way in Life, you can remember YOU again, the real you. All the goodness that was placed in you since the beginning of time will resurface. To the dreamer, you will dream again. To the discouraged, you will be encouraged. To the seemingly forgotten, you will be remembered. To the new you, you will rise and be the best version of yourself. To the poor in spirit, you will be rich through the awareness of your Creator. You will no longer be the same. Hey, new you, BE YOU

To my beautiful son, AJ, you inspired me. Your life's journey helped me to grow as a mom in the knowledge that I now have to nurture you along the way. My job is never over until I close my eyes.

Contents

Dedication iii

Do You Know Yourself? 2

SELF-ESTEEM 8

About The Author 22

*That's What I Like About Me is a follow-up book to the book **"Pretty Ain't So Pritty"** by author **Tasha Crews.** Through her writing and life experiences, she realized that human beings are stifled in their growth because of their perception of themselves. The Confidence Booklet was developed for people to see the best in themselves through vivid recollections of wonder-filled experiences through their interpersonal development. She desires people to realize that confidence is innate. We were all born with it! It simply began to fade through life experiences, thoughts, and emotions from environmental and social factors. Through a series of questions, she intrigues the participant to recall defining moments that remind them of this confidence that has already existed in them. So, one might ask, "What is the goal?" The goal is to encourage you to discover yourself, like yourself, and ultimately, LOVE yourself. It's one way to help others repeat these same activities and cause a chain reaction of humanity loving each other.*

The Self-Awareness and Self-Esteem

Let's recall. In THE CONFIDENCE BOOKLET, Making the self-discovery, you remembered something that you were good at along your journey. Now, let us expose some thoughts about becoming aware of YOU. I believe we should start with our creator first. Remember, ELOHIM? Remember, HE is the confidence distributor. He manufactured you. Therefore, he knows all about you. Now, you must get to know all about you.

God, Ellohim created you. You were only nurtured and transported to this great earth by your mother's womb. You were created with good intentions. The one who created you created you with LOVE from love. His intentions were that you stick close to him to know your existence and function on the earth. Picture yourself like Him! Remember those things in The Confidence Booklet? Some of those things were already a part of your makeup. If you had paid attention, you were building your consciousness. No worries, we are doing it right now. Simply put, pay attention to yourself and your God-given inner spirit, and you will begin to see who you are along with what you can do, be, or create.

Do You Know Yourself?

Are you one to be direct and honest or reserved and passive? Are you okay with sharing your thoughts, feelings, and emotions? Do you know what you like and what you don't like? Do you feel it's often easy for you to make final decisions? Have you ever wondered why you do certain things the way you do them? Do you ask yourself why you do things the way you do them? Do you put your right foot in your shoe first or your left foot in your shoe first? Do you hum when you chew? Do you notice when you are anxious? Do you notice what makes you calm? Do you space out in the middle of someone telling you a story? Ha Ha, we have all done it at some point. Do you tend to like happy movies? Do you enjoy being alone? Do you enjoy being around people? Lastly, are you attentive? Do you notice almost everything? These are all questions that will make you aware of yourself and who you just might be!

LET'S KEEP IT SIMPLE. OKAY?

LET'S DEFINE SELF-AWARENESS

Self-Awareness

Noun

- Conscious knowledge of one's own character, feelings, motives, and desires.
- "the process can be painful, but it leads to greater self-awareness."

- Oxford Languages

Knowing your character, feelings, motives, and desires can lead to greater self-awareness.

What Good Thoughts About Yourself Bring You Joy?

_____
_____
_____
_____
_____
_____
_____
_____
_____
_____
_____
_____

The Self-Awareness and Self-Esteem

Does Your Thoughts, Feelings, and Motives Towards Yourself Make You Feel Good About Yourself? Be Honest with You. Why?

***Here's a tip:** Do not judge your feelings. Simply state them. Then, reflect on them.*

_____
_____
_____
_____
_____
_____
_____
_____
_____
_____
_____
_____
_____
_____
_____
_____
_____
_____
_____
_____
_____
_____

TASHA CREWS

Name Three Things That You Will Work On.

The Self-Awareness and Self-Esteem

The best part of your life has just begun. By revisiting this Self-awareness section, you will start to identify things that make up the person you are or become. Remember, you can direct how you feel about yourself by knowing yourself. Be easy on yourself. Some things you can always change. Be optimistic about them. Get ready to like the changes that you are embarking upon. **GET READY TO LIKE YOU!**

TASHA CREWS

SELF-ESTEEM

How do you appreciate and value yourself?

Are you wondering why we didn't start with self-esteem? It is because, at an early age, it was being developed along the way externally. It is still being developed. Your self-esteem changes along the way with your experiences in life. Think about it. There are times when we don't " feel" our best, and there are times we feel great about ourselves. Not feeling our best should only be a temporary feeling. The exception now is that through self-awareness, you are directing where you'd like your self-esteem to be without those boundaries that were established "for you." Through self-awareness, you and no one else are determining where your self-esteem will be. Remember those exercises you did in THE SELF-CONFIDENCE BOOKLET? You were created with confidence first! Remember, fear did not exist. Now, let's talk about self-esteem.

Self-Esteem

Self-esteem is your overall opinion of yourself, your beliefs about your abilities, and your limitations.

Webber State University, Counseling and Psychological Services Center

The Self-Awareness and Self-Esteem

You have just completed your self-awareness section. You are aware and more knowledgeable about yourself. Let's combine what you have come to know and how you truly feel about this rediscovered knowledge about yourself. You see, what you know about yourself doesn't always reflect how you feel about yourself. This is one of the most important elements to keep yourself even existing at all!

Consider this statement, "true self-esteem is accessed through consistent information from your creator." He should first have access to your thoughts about you. Again, he created you. He has first-hand knowledge of you. Why go outside to another vendor in the world? God knows HIS work. Remember, you are his handiwork.

What Do You Think?

How Do You Define Self-Esteem? What Is Your Current Belief About Yourself?

Here's a tip: *Day in and day out, you complete many tasks consciously and unaware. In what areas do you believe you are capable of doing your best?*

<u>NAME THEM.</u>

1... 2... 3... GO!

_____
_____
_____
_____
_____
_____
_____
_____
_____
_____
_____
_____

The Self-Awareness and Self-Esteem

What Makes You Feel Good About You?

Describe How You Feel About Yourself.

Here's a tip: *START WITH, I feel good about myself when…*
(remember this is only about you talking to you!!)

_____
_____
_____
_____
_____
_____
_____
_____
_____
_____
_____
_____
_____
_____
_____
_____
_____
_____
_____
_____

Now That You Are Aware Of Some Things That You Feel Good About, Which One Are You Most Assured Of? Why? In Vivid Detail, Describe How Good You Are At That One Thing.

Here's a tip: " *I did a great job that time I………*

The Self-Awareness and Self-Esteem

Go ahead, speak well of yourself. It's OK to give yourself a boost when you need it. You are good at something. It is up to you to be confident in your God-given abilities. Your creator loves when you compliment what he does through you! Doesn't it feel good to acknowledge something good about yourself? How you feel about yourself can determine how many YESs you will give yourself versus the NOs you allow. Let's remove some of the unhealthy boundaries that keep you "there." Would you like to move?

TASHA CREWS

YOU TELL YOU, FIRST...

Remember, you were a misunderstood terrific two to what the world labeled as terrible. The only thing that is terrible is misunderstanding. Think about it. You were ready to explore. You found an item on the floor and tried to stick it in the socket!! You are very intelligent. You understood that the socket has three holes. Whatever was in your hand could possibly fit into one of the holes. Of course, that's not safe. But there were other times you felt you could climb the monkey bars on the playground. Remember you would try to swing your highest on the swings? Remember you would turn your fastest on the merry-go-round? How much excitement did you have?

Though you were too young to understand or care about the ramifications of life, you LIVED. Along the way, there was a pause and impediment to these wonderful feelings. Don't worry, and you can explore more along the way. Life inside you is not over. Later, you begin to be shaped by thoughts, experiences, relationships, culture, religion, and societal status. These are significant contributors to our self-esteem, according to a Webber State University Counseling and Psychological Services Center article.

The Self-Awareness and Self-Esteem

What if I told you that you are fearfully and wonderfully made? I didn't say it first. Maybe you have heard people say this in some religious setting. It comes from the Bible in the book of Psalms, chapter 139, verse 14. David, a man who was intimately devoted to spending time with his Creator, was discovering himself. That is how you find your value! Your self-esteem is an inward job! Your thoughts should be in sync with the one who created you. Sure, life happens. Sure, we have significant relationships and desire affirmations. Sure, we desire to make great accomplishments, but we should only measure our value and worth by truth. David goes on to say in verse 14, "Wonderful are your works, my soul knows it very well. Maybe you are not a bible reader. That's okay. But if someone told me something like that, I'd be floating on cloud nine. God's works are wonderful, and you are a part of that work. God knows the truth about you. Maybe you should too. Solidify your thoughts in God's word concerning you. Jesus also knows. Let's agree that you need to know. These biblical affirmations have helped many people to overcome low self-esteem to a more balanced self-esteem. Your thoughts are direct contributors to your self-esteem.

"As a man thinketh in his heart, so is he." Proverbs 23: 7

KEEP IT SIMPLE

We Will Focus On The Good Contributors. The Way You Think Of Yourself Will Affect How You Approach Life. Write 3 Good Thoughts About Yourself.

Here's a tip: *"I am a reliable worker," "I am a kind person," I am special because…*

_____
_____
_____
_____
_____
_____
_____
_____
_____
_____
_____
_____
_____
_____
_____

The Self-Awareness and Self-Esteem

REMEMBER:

Access The Good Thoughts About You Through Your Creator.

There are some people that bring out the best in you. How do you feel around them? Remember, we are talking about your feelings about you.

Since self-esteem is also shaped by culture, identify cultural ideals that agree with what God says about you.

Here's a tip: *What ideas, customs, and social behaviors that you take part in make you feel closer to what God says about you?*

_____
_____
_____
_____
_____
_____
_____
_____
_____
_____
_____
_____
_____
_____
_____
_____
_____

What Societal Status Are You Aiming for That Agrees with Your God-given Purpose or Talent?

Here's a tip: DOES what you want to do help others as well?

Finally, this book should be kept in a personal space that you can visit on a regular basis. Remember, confidence is built in you. It is your responsibility to not allow the outside influences to fade what you have and are building within. Your confidence existed long before you were aware. Stay tapped into it. Remove the illogical fears by replacing them with the rediscovered thoughts you have about yourself. Stay connected to Ellohim, the one who created you. When you do this, you are abiding, living beyond existing. After all, you were created with LOVE from love and with a function (purpose). There is more to be discovered about you and the things you will be, do, and create on this great earth that was created for you. **TAP IN!**

The Self-Awareness and Self-Esteem

To further your self-confidence, self-discovery, self-awareness, and self-esteem, you are invited to email Author and Confidence coach Tasha Crews at authortcrews@gmail.com for comments, blogs, events, and speaking engagements.

"Pretty Ain't So Pritty" Series Work Booklet two

About The Author

Tasha Crews is author of " Pretty Ain't So Pritty" and book series "That's What I Like About Me" : The Confidence Book and Self-Awareness to Self-Esteem. She is a native of North Carolina and Graduate of NCA&TSU. She is the proud mother of two children. She is a servant to her community where she serves as a community liason for various equity projects that serve marginalized and disenfranchised citizens. She is a community advocate and commentator for various local podcasts. She has been guest speaker for organizations As proud owner of COED ENTERTAINMENT TECH AND CONSULTING, she hosts seminars for low income communities that foster self development and reaching beyond the poverty line. She devotes her life to the Kingdom of God through Jesus, the Christ. She values all of God's creation and strives to increase self-awareness and self love among all humans in hopes of a better world for all people.